Writers

Janice Parker

Weigl

CALGARY

www.weigl.com

This series is dedicated to all Canadians who take pride in their communities and their citizenship; and to those who will continue to help build a strong Canada. The Canadians in this series have helped to build Canada by being outstanding in their fields, from literature to business, sports to the arts. Some have overcome great obstacles to make their dreams come true, and their dedication and achievement serve as an inspiration for young and old alike.

Published by Weigl Educational Publishers Limited
6325 – 10 Street SE
Calgary, Alberta, Canada
T2H 2Z9
Website: http://www.weigl.com

Canadian Cataloguing in Publication Data

Parker, Janice.
   Great Canadian writers

(Great Canadians)
Includes bibliographical references and index.
ISBN 1-896990-90-8

1. Authors, Canadian—Biography—Juvenile literature. I. Title.
II. Series: Great Canadians (Calgary, Alta.)
PS8081.P37 2000   jC810.9'005   C00-910050-4
PR9186.2.P37 2000

Printed and bound in Canada
1 2 3 4 5 6 7 8 9 0 04 03 02 01 00

Editor
Rennay Craats
Design
Warren Clark
Copy Editor
Heather Kissock
Layout
Lucinda Cage

Photograph Credits
Every reasonable effort has been made to trace ownership and to obtain permission to reprint copyright material. The publishers would be pleased to have any errors or omissions brought to their attention so that they may be corrected in subsequent printings

Ted Amsden: page 15; Ulf Andersen: page 43. Annick Press: page 26; Margaret Atwood: pages 7, 8, 9, 10; Jerry Bauer: page 18; Dan Coleman: page 45; CP Picture Archive: pages 11, 22, 23, 30, 35; John DeVisser: page 14; Globe and Mail (Barrie Davis): page 33; Neil Graham: page 36; HarperCollins: page 42, 44; Jerry Kopelow: page 41; Andrew MacNaughton: page 6; Michael Martchenko (from The Paper Bag Princess by Robert Munsch, reprinted with permission from Annick Press, ©1980): page 27; Montreal Gazette: pages 31, 32, 34; Farley Mowat: page 13; Munro Books: page 21; Bob Munsch Enterprises: cover, pages 24, 25, 28, 29; Nephew Photography: page 20; Paul Orenstein: page 12; Fred Phipps: page 16; Reuters/Peter Jones/Archive Photos: page 17; Carol Shields: pages 37, 38, 39, 40.

CONTENTS

6
Margaret Atwood

12
Farley Mowat

18
Alice Munro

24
Robert Munsch

30
Mordecai Richler

36
Carol Shields

MORE GREAT CANADIANS

Pierre Berton	42
Douglas Cooper	42
Douglas Coupland	42
Timothy Findley	42
Anne Hébert	43
Tomson Highway	43
Rita Joe	43
W.P. Kinsella	44
Joy Kogawa	44
Jean Little	44
Ann-Marie MacDonald	45
W.O. Mitchell	45
Michael Ondaatje	45
Glossary	46
Suggested Reading	47
Index	48

Writers

Canada is full of many talented writers. Canadians have been published and read long before Canada even became a country. The first Canadian writers wrote mostly about their explorations or travels across the country. These stories were usually in the form of diaries, reports, or letters. Later, stories were often written about Canada's landscape and its harsh winters or about the many animals that lived in the country.

By the twentieth century, there were many well-known Canadian authors. Lucy Maud Montgomery wrote her classic children's novel, *Anne of Green Gables*, in 1908. Another Canadian classic, *Sunshine Sketches of a Little Town*, was written by Stephen Leacock in 1912.

Canadian authors are known around the world. Many novelists today still write about their experiences of being born and raised in Canada. Margaret Laurence's *Stone Angel* and Robertson Davies' *Fifth Business* are just two examples of famous novels written by Canadian authors.

As a country with a history of welcoming immigrants, Canada has also had many writers who were born in other countries and who have chosen to make Canada their home. In their writings, these authors often compare their lives before and after coming to the country and comment on Canadian culture as a newcomer. For many people, novels, plays, and poetry written by Canadian writers reflect the culture of Canada. By reading these works, we can better understand what it means to be Canadian.

This book lists only a few of Canada's best writers, and it focusses on English-language writers. The suggested reading list at the back of the book gives sources where you can find out more about other Canadian writers, including the numerous French-language authors.

1939–

Margaret Atwood

> " I think I'm kind of an odd phenomenon in that I'm a serious writer and I never expected to become a popular one, and I never did anything in order to become a popular one. "

Key Events

1961 Receives E.J. Pratt Medal for *Double Persephone*

1961 Graduates with a bachelor of arts degree from the University of Toronto

1966 Receives Governor General's Award for *The Circle Game*

1973 Named Officer of the Order of Canada

1981 Named Companion of the Order of Canada

1986 Receives Governor General's Award for *The Handmaid's Tale*

1996 Wins Giller Prize for *Alias Grace*

Early Years

Born in Ottawa, Margaret was the middle child in her family. Her mother was independent and an excellent storyteller. Margaret's father was a zoology professor who specialized in studying insects. During the first few years of her life, Margaret often travelled with her family to wherever her father was doing research. During this time, the Atwoods lived in the wilderness, in tents, and then later in a cabin.

At a young age, Margaret learned how to canoe, catch and scale fish, and use guns and bows and arrows. Margaret only attended school during the winter months because her family spent so many months in the bush. She did not attend school full time until she was in the eighth grade.

When Margaret's family lived in the wilderness, books were often the only entertainment for the children. Fortunately, Margaret liked to read. She especially loved stories about dragons and magic, Grimm's fairy tales, and comic books. Margaret also wrote some poetry, or "scribbles," as she calls them, between the ages of five and seven. After that, she did not write at all until she was sixteen, when she decided she wanted to become a writer.

Even as a young girl, Margaret loved to read and write. Her life in the bush gave her plenty to write about.

Backgrounder

Grimm's Fairy Tales

Written in the nineteenth century by two German brothers, Jakob and Wilhelm Grimm, Grimm's fairy tales are still read to and by children today. Many of the tales are very famous, such as "Little Red Riding Hood," "Snow White," "Cinderella," and "Sleeping Beauty." Some of the stories were published before the Grimm's collection, but most were collected from the brothers' friends in Germany. By publishing the stories, the Grimm brothers hoped that the tales would live on for years.

Developing Skills

After high school, Margaret studied English at the University of Toronto. University opened Margaret's eyes. For the first time, she realized that many Canadians were writing poetry and novels and being published. By the time she graduated, she had published her first book of poetry and won an award for it.

From Toronto, Margaret went on to earn a master's degree at Harvard University in the United States. Like many students, Margaret waited until the last moment to finish her papers. Despite this, she was a hard worker. When she was not doing schoolwork, she was writing poetry.

Margaret was not entirely happy at Harvard. Female students were not treated the same as male students. Only male students, for example, were allowed into the library that held a large collection of modern poetry. Living in the United States also made Margaret realize that Canadian writing was different from American writing. By the time she left Harvard, Margaret was certain that she would be a proudly Canadian writer.

As a child, Margaret mastered the art of canoeing. As an adult, she still enjoys exploring nature.

After completing her studies at Harvard, Margaret spent the summer with a friend in England. She also travelled throughout France. In autumn, Margaret returned to Canada. She got a job as an instructor at the University of British Columbia. The year she spent in Vancouver was very productive. Margaret enjoyed teaching. She also wrote fourteen stories and many new poems, created a draft of one novel, and started two others.

All of this hard work was exhausting for Margaret. Her health suffered. Despite this, she submitted her writing to publishers. The following year, Margaret returned to study at Harvard.

Margaret's second book of poetry, *The Circle Game*, was first published in 1964. It was a great success. *The Circle Game* won the Governor General's Award in 1966. Margaret was truly a well-known writer now. She was frequently interviewed by the media as well. She was approached by several publishers who wanted to work with her. By this time, Margaret had finished writing her first novel.

> *As an artist, your first loyalty is to your art. Unless this is the case, you're going to be a second-rate artist.*

The Circle Game was one of five volumes of poetry Margaret released between 1966 and 1971.

Backgrounder

The Order of Canada

The Order of Canada was first awarded during Canada's centennial in 1967. It is the highest honour that a Canadian can receive. Appointments to the Order are announced twice each year. The appointees are people who have made a difference to the country during their lifetime. There are three levels of the Order of Canada: member, officer, and companion. Members are people who have made a difference at a local or regional level. Officers are recognized for their contributions to the country. Companions of the Order are recognized for outstanding achievement in their field at the national or international level. Margaret was made both an Officer and a Companion of the Order of Canada.

Accomplishments

Margaret submitted her first novel, *The Edible Woman*, to a publisher in 1965. She did not hear from the publisher for two years. It seemed as though the publisher had misplaced the **manuscript**. After Margaret won the Governor General's Award, the publisher found the manuscript and began to work on it. *The Edible Woman* was published in 1969, while Margaret was teaching at the University of Alberta.

For the next several years, Margaret taught at various universities and continued to write. Although most of her works are poetry or novels, she did other types of writing as well. *The Journals of Susanna Moodie* was a **non-fiction** book that pulled together writings of a famous Canadian female writer who had lived in the nineteenth century. Margaret felt that she had something in common with Susanna Moodie, who had also spent a lot of time outdoors. Margaret drew and painted pictures that appeared in the book.

As well as writing non-fiction, Margaret wrote plays for radio and television and was the editor of many other books on Canadian literature. After the birth of her daughter, Jess, Margaret began writing children's books. *Up in the Tree* was her first book for children. Margaret drew the pictures and wrote out the words by hand for the book. *Anna's Pet*, written with Margaret's aunt, is about a young girl who digs up worms.

Margaret dedicated *Up in the Tree* to her daughter, Jess. Margaret enjoyed the happy endings in children's literature.

As well as writing many different types of books, Margaret is able to write in many different styles. In 1985, she wrote a novel called *The Handmaid's Tale*. This **science fiction** novel is about how women may be treated in the future. The book won a Governor General's Award in 1986 and was also made into a movie.

Margaret's 1996 novel *Alias Grace* is based on a historical crime that occurred in Canada. Grace Marks, the woman in the book, is accused of killing her employer. Margaret used as many facts about the case as she could find in old newspapers and other sources. She also made up much of the book. The novel won the Giller Prize.

Margaret has had a very busy writing career. She has written more than forty books including novels, books of poetry, and many other works. She is also quite active in trying to help other writers. She has been chair of the Writers' Union of Canada and president of the Anglo-Canadian chapter of PEN International. Margaret once joked that she helps out so many organizations because as a Brownie, she was trained to work for good causes.

> **"** *Every once in a while, I feel that I want to write a book about outer space where there's nothing but ray guns and monsters.* **"**

Margaret found out everything she could about Grace Marks to write her novel *Alias Grace*.

Backgrounder

PEN

PEN is an international writer's group that believes that writers should be allowed to express themselves freely. PEN stands for "poets, playwrights, editors, essayists, and novelists." The organization helps defend writers who are jailed or who suffer **oppression** from their governments. PEN also gives out literary awards and helps translate literary works. To become a member of PEN, a writer usually must have published at least two books.

1921–

Farley Mowat

> 66 A good book for youngsters can influence the whole life of the young reader. I believe that it is an absolute duty for good writers to spend a significant part of their time and talent writing for young people. 99

Key Events

1935   Travels to the Arctic with his uncle

1939   Joins the Canadian army

1952   Publishes *People of the Deer*

1957   Receives Governor General's Award for *Lost in the Barrens*

1963   Releases *Never Cry Wolf*

1981   Is appointed Officer of the Order of Canada

1987   Writes biography, *Woman in the Mists: The Story of Dian Fossey and the Mountain Gorillas of Africa*

Early Years

An only child, Farley was always a bit different from other children. He was too small to play most sports. Other children often made fun of his name and he spent a great deal of time alone.

Farley's love of animals kept him from being lonely. From the time he was a young child, he was interested in nature. He had many different pets, including a dog, a great horned owl, and a black squirrel. He also kept rats and snakes. Farley especially liked studying birds.

During his childhood, Farley and his parents moved to several different cities. When Farley was about twelve, they moved to Saskatoon. Farley started a naturalist's club that published a magazine called *Nature Lore*. He also wrote articles for the children's section of the local newspaper.

When the Mowats later moved to Toronto, Farley joined the Toronto Ornithological Field Group and wrote for their newsletter. From 1939 to 1946, Farley was in the Canadian Armed Forces. By the time he returned from fighting in Italy during World War II, he had been promoted to captain.

Farley joined the army because his father had been a soldier in World War I. Farley could never forget his terrible experiences in combat.

Backgrounder

Ornithology

Ornithology is the science of studying birds. Ornithologists learn much about birds by observing them in the wild, often with binoculars. Bird banding is also used to tell us about the movements of birds during migration.

Developing Skills

Even while he was serving in the army in Italy, Farley continued to write. He began writing the original version of what would eventually become *The Dog Who Wouldn't Be*. He also sent articles to be published in *Maclean's* magazine.

When he returned to Canada after the war, Farley began to plan for the future. He enrolled at the University of Toronto. He now knew that he was most interested in becoming a writer. Farley also wanted to return to the Arctic. When he was about fourteen, Farley had accompanied his biologist uncle on a trip to Churchill, Manitoba, to watch the migration of the caribou.

Soon, Farley had the chance to assist a field scientist in collecting specimens from the Keewatin district in northern Canada. The following summer, he returned to the Arctic as a government biologist to study caribou and wolves. Farley was supposed to learn whether wolves were responsible for the disappearance of the caribou. After studying the animals for many hours, he came to the conclusion that wolves only ate the old or very sick caribou. The wolves ate mostly field mice. From the experiences of his two summers in the Arctic, Farley found material for several of his books.

Farley always loved animals. He spent a lot of time with his Newfoundland water dog, Albert.

Backgrounder

Churchill, Manitoba
Churchill is located in northern Manitoba on Hudson's Bay. Churchill is a very good place to observe different kinds of birds and animals. Many polar bears spend part of the year near Churchill as they wait for the ice to freeze so that they can travel further north. The area has become a popular place for tourists to visit and view the bears.

Farley's first book began as a short story. In *People of the Deer,* he wrote about an Inuit tribe that lived near the area of his wolf studies. Farley discovered that the Inuit were starving because the caribou were dying off. He felt that the government was not doing enough to help the Inuit. He also wanted the rest of Canada to know what was happening. Farley became well-known with this book. Many people disagreed with his views, but Farley was credited with bringing increased awareness about the people living in the Arctic to the rest of Canada.

A few years after *People of the Deer* was published, Farley wrote his first of many novels for younger readers, *Lost in the Barrens.* This book received the Governor General's Award. Although the book was **fiction**, it was based somewhat on Farley's life. Like Farley, the fourteen-year-old character travels to Northern Canada with his uncle.

Only one year after publishing his first children's book, Farley published another. In *The Dog Who Wouldn't Be*, Farley wrote about many of the funny things that happened with his childhood dog, Mutt.

" *I experience and observe, and then I write.* "

Many of Farley's books explore the future of wild animals.

Accomplishments

Farley's wolf research led to his book, *Never Cry Wolf*, which became a bestseller. The book was **translated** and sold around the world. In the book, Farley argued that wolves were not vicious killers. Instead, they ate mostly small mammals, such as mice, and they only ate enough to stay alive. The wolves rarely killed larger animals such as caribou. *Never Cry Wolf* changed opinions worldwide about wolves. In Russia, for example, the government banned the killing of wolves in the wild.

Farley wrote other books to educate people about wild animals. *Sea of Slaughter* is about animals in the North Atlantic that have become **extinct** or **endangered**. Humans are responsible for the disappearance of these animals because of pollution, loss of habitat, and hunting. With the book, Farley hoped to convince people that they must work to save endangered animals.

Farley's reputation as an environmentalist led him to write a book he had not planned on writing. After gorilla researcher Dian Fossey was murdered in 1985, a publisher asked Farley to write a book about her life. At first, Farley refused. He had never written a book for someone else before. After reading some of Dian's letters and diary entries, however, Farley became more interested. Like Farley, Dian was outspoken about trying to help animals. Farley decided to write the **biography** about Dian using many of her own writings. The book was later made into a movie.

Farley's trips to the Arctic inspired his best-known works.

Backgrounder

Dian Fossey

Dian Fossey was a scientist who went to Africa to study **primates,** especially mountain gorillas, in 1966. She started a research centre in Rwanda, and lived there until she was murdered in her cabin in 1985. Dian's murder was never solved. In his book about her life, Farley helped people understand Dian and her efforts to save gorillas from extinction.

> 66 *The essence of good writing is storytelling and it's oral and always has been and will remain so. And if we lose touch with that, we become incompetent as writers.* 99

Farley's 1998 book *Farfarers: Before the Norse* is drawn from a lifetime of research as a naturalist and biologist. It tells the story of the forgotten people of the Hudson Bay area.

Farley also wrote an **autobiography** about his own childhood, *Born Naked*. He describes himself as a child who had more in common with animals than with other people. The book also tells how Farley fell in love with nature and the Arctic.

Farley no longer believes that he can save nature or animals from extinction. He has said that "in the end, my crusades have accomplished nothing. I haven't saved the wolf, the whales, the seals, primitive man, or the outpost people." Farley believes that humans will continue to make bad choices about the environment.

Farley continues to write books. Although some people consider him a nature writer, he believes that he is, above all, a storyteller. His books for adults and children continue to captivate readers all over the world.

▶▶▶▶▶▶

QUICK NOTES

▶ Farley has a scar on the back of his right hand where he was bitten by a rattlesnake.

▶ As a child, Farley spent many hours in the libraries where his father worked as a librarian.

▶ Farley's books have been translated into more than thirty different languages. He has sold more than 14 million books worldwide.

1931–

Alice Munro

> **"** I never intended to be a short story writer. I started writing them because I didn't have time to write anything else—I had three children. And then I got used to writing stories, so I saw my material that way, and I don't think I'll ever write a novel. **"**

Key Events

1951 Marries James Munro

1952 Receives her bachelor of arts degree from the University of Western Ontario

1969 Receives Governor General's Award for *Dance of the Happy Shades*

1976 Divorces James Munro and marries Gerald Fremlin, whom she met at university

1979 Receives Governor General's Award for *The Beggar Maid: Stories of Flo and Rose*

1987 Receives Governor General's Award for *The Progress of Love*

1990 Publishes *Friend of My Youth*

1994 Publishes *Open Secrets*

1998 Wins Giller Prize for *The Love of a Good Woman*

Early Years

Ever since she was a young girl in Wingham, Ontario, Alice knew she wanted to be a famous writer. She wanted to be like Emily after reading Lucy Maud Montgomery's *Emily of New Moon*. It is a story about a young girl who aspires to become a writer. Alice began to write stories when she was a teenager.

When Alice was an adolescent, her mother developed **Parkinson's disease**. Soon, her mother was not able to help around the house. Alice, the eldest of three children, took over the tasks of cooking, washing, and ironing for the family until her grandmother and an aunt came to help. Despite these hardships, Alice was confident and did well in school. But her situation did not give her much time to write. She began spending her lunch hours in high school writing.

Alice dreamed of going to university, but her family did not have the money to send her. She knew that if she got the best marks in her class, she would win a **scholarship** that would pay for her first two years. Luckily, Alice was an excellent student. She worked hard and won the scholarship.

Alice's life in Wingham, Ontario, influenced her writing.

Backgrounder

Lucy Maud Montgomery

Maud, as she liked to be called, was one of Canada's most celebrated authors. Born on Prince Edward Island in 1874, Maud began to write at the age of nine. She dreamed of becoming a great writer. When she finished school, Maud became a teacher. She continued to write mostly poetry. Maud wrote her first novel in 1908. This book, *Anne of Green Gables*, went on to become one of the bestselling books of all time. People all over the world fell in love with the unstoppable, red-haired Anne.

Developing Skills

Alice continued to write while in university. In 1950, she had one of her stories published in the university's student magazine. At university, Alice also met her husband Jim. After her second year of university, the two married and moved to Vancouver.

Alice worked at the Vancouver Public Library, and she and Jim soon began a family. To most people, Alice appeared to lead the life of a typical homemaker. She cooked and watched over the house, raised her children, and worked part-time to help support her family. All the while, however, Alice was secretly writing whenever she could find time. Only her husband, who always encouraged her to write, knew that this was how she spent her few spare moments.

With other people, Alice would make up reasons why she was so busy at home. She often said she was sewing curtains.

Alice wanted to write a novel, but she found she was too busy with her children. She found it easier to write short stories. Alice always believed that her short stories were just practice for writing a novel. By the time she turned thirty, Alice was disappointed that she had not become an accomplished writer. She decided to act on her husband's suggestion to rent an office so she could dedicate herself to writing. When the children were in school, Alice went to the office and tried to write a novel. For eight months, she wrote almost nothing. Alice became frustrated.

Many of Alice's stories follow the lives of characters who live in small Canadian towns.

Alice and Jim decided to pack up their family and move to Victoria. They started their own business—a bookstore called Munro's Books. Both worked very hard to make the store successful. With the responsibilities of the business and raising a family, Alice realized that she was too busy to write longer works. Instead, she continued to write short stories. She found it easier to write once she stopped pressuring herself to write a novel. These years were full of hard work, but they were very happy times for Alice and her family.

> *I would have given up anything to be a writer when I was a teenager. I'd have given up boyfriends. I'd have given up the whole of ordinary life to make this other world.*

By this time, Alice's stories were being read on CBC radio and published in magazines such as *Chatelaine*. A publisher wanted to put out a book of her stories even though she was not a well-known writer. Alice was thrilled. She gathered together many of the stories she had written in the previous fourteen years. She even wrote three new stories for the collection. Her book of stories, called *Dance of the Happy Shades*, was published in 1968. The following year, Alice won a Governor General's Award for the book. She was finally getting her wish of becoming a famous writer.

Alice's love for books led to the family business—Munro's Books.

Backgrounder

Governor General's Literary Awards

Every year, Canadian authors, illustrators, and translators who have published a book are eligible to win a Governor General's Literary Award. Awards of $10,000 each are given in several different categories. Other writers judge who should be the winners.

Accomplishments

After winning the Governor General's Award, Alice finally admitted to herself and others that she was a writer. When a **census** taker asked about her occupation, for the first time Alice wrote down "writer" instead of "housewife." She continued to write at home. Alice never liked writing in an office. She wrote much of her next book, *Lives of Girls and Women*, in the laundry room because it was the warmest room in the house.

Alice's second book sold even more copies than her first. Around this period, Alice at times believed that she would stop writing. She felt that she had no more short story ideas. As it turned out, she continued to write as steadily as ever.

As Alice attained more success as a writer, her family life became more difficult. She and her husband Jim decided that they would separate. The next year, Alice and her two youngest daughters moved to Ontario, where Alice took a position as writer-in-residence at the University of Western Ontario in London.

▶▶▶▶▶▶

QUICK NOTES

▶ *Lives of Girls and Women* was made into a television movie for CBC.
▶ Alice has acted in plays at a theatre near her home.
▶ Some people in her hometown were upset by *Lives of Girls and Women*. They thought the book's characters were based on Wingham citizens. Alice assured everyone that her book was fiction.

Alice does not tie her stories up neatly at the end. She leaves readers to draw their own conclusions.

Alice's personal life became happier. She married Gerald Fremlin, a geographer whom she had known in university. The couple moved to an area in Ontario close to where they had both grown up.

Writing is very important to Alice. She cannot imagine not constantly writing. She has a reputation for writing beautiful stories about ordinary people living in small towns in Canada. Alice often writes stories about the area in which she grew up. Fans of her stories wait eagerly for her next book to appear.

Alice also continues to win literary prizes for her writing. She is perhaps the best-known short story writer in Canada and North America. In 1998, she won the Giller Prize for *The Love of a Good Woman*.

> " I would never give my work to anyone to read. I have too little confidence—not the real confidence to be a writer. "

Alice has received many awards. In 1999, America's National Book Critics Circle awarded its 1999 fiction prize to Alice for *The Love of a Good Woman*.

Backgrounder

The Giller Prize

Every year since 1994, the Giller Prize has been given to the author of the best Canadian novel or collection of short stories written in English. The author also receives $25,000. The Giller Prize was founded by a Toronto businessman, Jack Rabinovitch. He named the prize in honour of his late wife, Doris Giller, a literary journalist.

1945–
Robert Munsch

> **"** I just keep telling stories and see which ones turn out. The story doesn't usually get good until I have told it about 100 times. **"**

Key Events

1973   Marries Ann Beeler

1975   Immigrates to Canada

1979   Publishes *Mud Puddle* and *The Dark*

1980   Publishes *The Paper Bag Princess*

1983   Becomes a Canadian citizen

1986   Publishes *Love You Forever*, the year's bestselling children's book in Canada and the United States

1991   Receives the Canadian Booksellers Association Author of the Year Award

Early Years

Canada's best-known children's storyteller was actually born in Pittsburgh, Pennsylvania. Bob came from a very large family—he was the fourth of nine children. Bob was very intelligent, but he hated school. He could not spell, disliked math, and did not like to work in groups. Teachers noticed that Bob would rarely pay attention during class. He spent most of his time in school daydreaming.

Bob became much happier after he started to read. He read all the time, taking book after book out of the library. One summer, he read more than 200 books. As early as elementary school, Bob wrote poetry.

By high school, Bob was a good student—his favourite subject was history. He did not have many friends, and preferred to stay home alone to read science fiction books and listen to classical music. Bob decided what he wanted to do with his life. He decided that he wanted to become a Jesuit Priest. He also studied history and **anthropology** at university.

Bob was the middle child. He had to battle both the younger and the older "gang" of siblings.

Backgrounder

Jesuits

Jesuits are an order of Roman Catholic priests. A Jesuit is also called a member of the Society of Jesus. The Jesuits have been around since the sixteenth century. They are known for their educational and missionary work and for their charity.

Developing Skills

While he was studying to become a priest, Bob was given the choice of taking philosophy lessons or working part time at an orphanage. He chose the orphanage. The orphanage had 800 children and very few nuns to care for them. Bob spent a lot of time with the children, often just talking.

After seven years, Bob decided to leave the Jesuits. He did not know what to do with his life, but he knew he liked to work with children. Bob went to work at a day care while he figured out what else to do. With children, Bob finally had an outlet for all his daydreaming. In order to calm the children down, he would make up stories to tell them. Some of the stories were not very good. Others were very popular with the children.

Bob got many ideas for stories from the children at the day care. He would tell the same stories over and over again. Each time, he would listen to what the children liked, and he would make small changes. Bob often used the children's suggestions in his stories.

When Bob and his wife, Ann, both lost their day care jobs, they decided to move to Canada. They went to Guelph, Ontario, where Bob got a job as a professor and also worked at the university day care telling stories.

Bob took a job in a day care while he figured out what he wanted to do. He found that he wanted to work in day care!

One day, the wife of Bob's boss overheard Bob telling stories in the day care. She was a children's librarian, and she knew that his stories would make wonderful books. Her husband gave Bob two months off with pay to write down his stories. Bob wrote ten stories and sent them to ten different publishers. One publisher liked his book *Mud Puddle* and decided to publish it. Bob's book *The Dark* was also published the same year.

Although these first two books did not sell many copies, Bob's publisher wanted another story from him. His next book, *The Paper Bag Princess*, sold many copies. Michael Martchenko, who illustrated the book, has illustrated many of Bob's other books. *The Paper Bag Princess* is a good example of what Bob calls his "anti-fairy tales." The heroine of the story uses her brains to outsmart a dragon and save a helpless prince. The book made enough money that Bob was able to quit his teaching job. He could finally do full time what he loved to do most—write and tell stories to children.

After the success of *The Paper Bag Princess*, Bob quit his job to write full time.

> 66 *I always used kids from storytelling in my books. The first kid who was in a story sort of "owned" the story and would get to be the kid in the book—if the story ever got to be a book.* 99

Backgrounder

Michael Martchenko

Michael is an illustrator who is best known for his drawings in many of Robert Munsch's books. Born in France, Michael moved with his family to Canada when he was seven. He has won many awards for his illustrations, including several for books written by Bob.

Accomplishments

As a full-time storyteller, Bob travels and tells his stories to children everywhere. He sometimes tells stories to as many as 3,000 children at once. Although many children get to hear him in large theatres, Bob is more comfortable with small audiences. Bob especially likes telling stories to groups of children at schools and day cares.

Bob receives many invitations from students asking him to come to their schools. Sometimes he shows up at a school unannounced. He often surprises the children and teachers by telling stories for the day. Once, Bob visited a second grade class in the United States. He said, "Hi, I'm Bob Munsch. Remember you asked me to come and visit when you wrote me last year?" At first, the teacher did not believe that the visitor was *the* Robert Munsch. Finally, she told her students to drop everything they were doing so that they could listen to Bob's stories.

While on book tours, Bob often stops in to visit classes who have written to him.

Backgrounder

Fan Letters

Bob receives 10,000 letters from children every year. Bob loves this fan mail and tries to answer the letters. Sometimes Bob visits schools or children who have written to him. He often gets story ideas from the letters he receives.

> 66 I became a writer so kids could hear my stories even if I was not telling them. 99

Bob makes up new stories in front of his audiences. If they like the stories, he talks to his publisher about making books out of them.

When Bob travels, he likes to stay with families that have young children instead of in hotels. At first, he did this because he could not afford to stay in hotels. Now, he simply prefers to get to know the people in a community. This way, he makes new friends and often gets new story ideas from the children. Bob also gets story ideas from children who write to him. One young girl sent Bob a story about her family's move to Canada from Lebanon. Bob wrote a book about her experiences.

Bob is now one of the most popular children's authors in North America. His books have sold more than 28 million copies. *Love You Forever* is the best-selling children's picture book ever in North America. It has sold 8 million copies!

▶▶▶▶▶▶
QUICK NOTES

▶ Bob has his own web site (www. robertmunsch.com), where he tells about his life and writing.

▶ Each of Bob's three children is in one of his books: Julie is in *David's Father*, Tyya is in *Something Good*, and Andrew is in *Andrew's Loose Tooth*.

▶ At first, Bob did not think that his storytelling skills were anything special. As he says, "Most of the other teachers made better playdough."

1931–

Mordecai Richler

> **"** Like any serious writer, I want to write one novel that will last, something that will keep me remembered after death, so I'm compelled to keep trying. **"**

Key Events

1951 Moves to Paris

1954 Publishes first novel, *The Acrobats,* published as *Wicked We Love*

1959 Publishes *The Apprenticeship of Duddy Kravitz*

1960 Marries Florence Wood

1968 Wins Governor General's Award for *Cocksure*

1971 Wins Governor General's Award for *St. Urbain's Horseman*

1974 Nominated for an Academy Award for the screenplay version of *The Apprenticeship of Duddy Kravitz*

1975 Publishes *Jacob Two-Two Meets the Hooded Fang*

1980 Publishes *Joshua Then and Now*

1985 Film version of *Joshua Then and Now* comes out

1992 Publishes *Oh Canada! Oh Quebec! Requiem for a Divided Country*

1997 Wins Giller Prize for *Barney's Version*

Early Years

Mordecai grew up on St. Urbain Street in a poor area of Montreal. As a young child, he read mostly comic books, such as *Captain Marvel* and *Batman*. He later began to read Ellery Queen and Perry Mason mysteries. When he was twelve, he read *All Quiet on the Western Front*.

Mordecai's family were Orthodox Jews. This meant that he had to study Hebrew and take religion classes three days a week after school. When Mordecai was about fifteen, his parents divorced.

Mordecai was not a good student in high school. Despite this, he went to university for two years to study English. During this time, he also worked part time for the *Montreal Herald* newspaper. Mordecai disliked university as much as high school. He dropped out and went to Europe. He decided that he would live in Paris and try to write.

Mordecai cashed in an insurance policy his mother had taken out on him and went to Europe. He wanted to see if he could write.

Backgrounder

Montreal

Montreal is the largest city in Quebec. About two-thirds of people in the city speak French. The area that is now Montreal was named Mont Real (Mount Royal) in 1535 by the explorer Jacques Cartier. Today, while most of the people living in Montreal are Catholic, there is also a large population of Protestants. About three percent of people in Montreal are Jewish.

Developing Skills

While living in Paris, Mordecai spent time with many other authors, such as Mavis Gallant and Allen Ginsberg. Mordecai wrote his first novel, *The Acrobat*, while he was there. Very soon, he ran out of money and had to return home to Canada. Mordecai worked at many different jobs and had his book published.

Mordecai did not remain in Canada for long. Within a year, he had decided to move to London, England, and write full time. Mordecai's next novel, *The Apprenticeship of Duddy Kravitz*, was written and published in 1959.

The book is about a poor young Jewish man who grows up in Montreal and wants to become a financial success. The characters grow up in the same neighbourhood that Mordecai grew up in.

During the next few years, Mordecai wrote several other novels. He quickly became known as a talented author and **satirist**. In addition to his novels, Mordecai wrote articles for magazines in Canada, the United States, and Great Britain. He also wrote many screenplays for radio and television.

> " I still work on a typewriter. I don't know anything about computers and I have no interest in knowing anything about computers. "

Mordecai felt that he found his writing style while creating Duddy Kravitz. The gradual success of that book gave Mordecai confidence in his ability.

Mordecai wrote about another Jewish-Canadian main character in his novel, *Joshua, Then and Now*. Like many of the characters in Mordecai's books, Joshua is not very likeable. Despite this, readers found the book very humorous and the novel was a great success.

In 1975, Mordecai wrote his first children's book, *Jacob Two-Two Meets the Hooded Fang*. The book's main character, six-year-old Jacob, says everything twice. Jacob defeats the Hooded Fang and saves other children who have been imprisoned.

Jacob Two-Two was an instant hit with children and **critics** alike. Mordecai was surprised at the popularity of the book. It sold more than any of his adult novels. *Jacob Two-Two* was translated into several different languages and was made into a musical and a film. Mordecai wrote two other books based on the character of Jacob: *Jacob Two-Two and the Dinosaur*, and *Jacob Two-Two's First Spy Case*.

The success of *Jacob Two-Two* surprised Mordecai. It almost embarrassed him. The hardcopy children's book outsold his most successful adult novel.

Backgrounder

Writing for Children

Before writing *Jacob Two-Two*, Mordecai had considered the idea of writing a book for children. He did not actually write the book until a year later because he disliked many children's books. He said, "I decided if I ever got around to writing a book for my kids, its intention would be to amuse. Pure fun, not instruction, is what I had in mind." With *Jacob Two-Two*, Mordecai succeeded in writing a book that was pure fun.

Accomplishments

Mordecai usually takes many years to write a novel. His 1989 book *Solomon Gursky was Here* was published nine years after his previous novel. The story is about a Jewish writer who is obsessed with writing a biography of Solomon Gursky.

In between publishing novels, Mordecai usually writes many magazine articles and non-fiction books. His *Home Sweet Home: My Canadian Album* is a collection of essays written about Mordecai's childhood in Montreal. The book also examines many Canadian traditions, such as hockey.

Mordecai's next non-fiction book about Canada, *Oh Canada! Oh Quebec*, caused quite a stir when it was published. The book is full of Mordecai's opinions about Quebec wanting to separate from the rest of Canada. Many people felt the book was too negative toward Quebec. One Canadian politician even wanted the book to be banned.

Mordecai has won a great many awards for his writing, including the Commonwealth Writers Prize and the Governor General's Award.

Backgrounder

Quebec Separatism

Many people in the province of Quebec believe that Quebec should separate from the rest of Canada and become its own political entity. Separatists feel that Quebec is very different from the rest of Canada, especially in language and culture. They believe that the Québécois would be better off if they were not part of the rest of English-speaking Canada.

This Year in Jerusalem tells about the year Mordecai lived in Israel. In the book, Mordecai also writes about the experience of being Jewish in Canada. Like *Home Sweet Home*, this book contains many of Mordecai's memories of growing up in Montreal, when his grandfather had been a respected rabbi. One critic described *This Year in Jerusalem* as "history made personal."

In 1997, Mordecai published another novel, *Barney's Version*. This novel tells about a man with **Alzheimer's disease**. The character wants to write his autobiography before he loses his memory. Like many of Mordecai's novels, *Barney's Version* is set in Montreal. *Barney's Version* won Mordecai the Giller Prize.

> ❝ I never outline a book. If you knew what was going to happen, it would be too boring. ❞

> ▶▶▶▶▶▶
>
> ## QUICK NOTES
>
> ▶ *Jacob Two-Two Meets the Hooded Fang* was inspired by a bedtime story that Mordecai told his youngest child, Jacob.
>
> ▶ Two of Mordecai's five children are also writers. His eldest son, Daniel, a television broadcaster, has written a novel called *Kicking Tomorrow*. The youngest, Jacob, writes for magazines.

Mordecai writes more than books. He also writes articles for national magazines, including *Saturday Night*.

1935–

Carol Shields

> **66** My kind of writer doesn't get famous. We just get more mail, more phone calls, more requests to do things. **99**

Key Events

1957   Marries Donald Shields

1965   Wins CBC young writer's contest

1972   Publishes her first book of poetry, *Others*

1975   Receives her master's degree in Canadian literature

1985   Publishes *Various Miracles,* her first collection of short stories

1994   Receives Governor General's Award for *The Stone Diaries*

1995   Wins Pulitzer Prize

1998   Is appointed an Officer of the Order of Canada

Early Years

Carol had a happy childhood. She grew up in Oak Park, Illinois, which is the same suburb where American author Ernest Hemingway was born. Even as a young child, she loved reading.

After graduating from high school, Carol studied at Hanover College in Indiana. She spent one of her college years as an exchange student in England. There she met a Canadian engineering student named Donald Shields. After graduating, Carol married Donald and the couple moved to Vancouver.

Although Carol wanted to write, she had little time to do so seriously. Her first priority was her growing family. After having children, Carol realized that she loved being a mother. In all, Carol and Donald had five children. Once the children grew older, Carol was able to devote more time to her writing. When she was thirty, she entered and won a national poetry contest. Her poem was read on CBC Radio.

Carol (right) was born in Chicago, Illinois, and grew up in Oak Park, Illinois.

Backgrounder

CBC

The Canadian Broadcasting Corporation—or CBC—produces Canada's national radio and television stations. There are many different stations to watch and listen to today, but the CBC has been especially important to Canadians. The CBC has always supported Canadian writers and television programs.

Developing Skills

It would be many years before Carol would have any of her work published. Instead, she and her family moved to Ottawa, where her husband worked at the university. Carol decided to return to university to get a master's degree in Canadian literature.

> *I was writing exactly what I wanted to write, not what would sell. Writing wasn't a career. It was just what I did.*

Two of Carol's professors encouraged her to make a collection of her poetry. *Others*, Carol's first book of poems, was published in 1972. Two years later, Carol had a second book of poetry, called *Intersect*, published. Carol decided to take a year off from her studies to write a novel. Many publishers rejected her first novel. This did not discourage Carol. She set out to write a second novel, *Small Ceremonies*, which was her first published novel. It came out in 1976, when Carol was forty years old. The main character in this novel is an ordinary homemaker. Carol had three other novels published during the next six years.

Carol studied at Hanover College, the University of Exeter in England, and the University of Ottawa, where she received a master's degree.

Carol continued to write steadily, publishing more novels and plays. Although her early novels were popular with readers, literary critics did not take her seriously. She was criticized for writing "women's books" and was told that her stories were "smaller than life." Carol did not let the criticism bother her. She continued to write exactly what she wanted to write.

Carol started to take more chances with her writing. She tried writing in different styles. In 1985, she published her first collection of short stories, *Various Miracles*. She still wrote about ordinary people's lives, but her writing style became more adventurous. She wrote a mystery in 1987 in which the story is told by several different characters. The book *Swann: A Mystery* won the Arthur Ellis Award as the best Canadian crime novel. A few years later, Carol wrote a romance novel called *The Republic of Love*.

Carol balanced her active family with her dreams of becoming an award-winning writer.

Backgrounder

Arthur Ellis Awards

The Crime Writers of Canada Association gives Arthur Ellis Awards to authors who write about crime. Every year since 1984, the awards have honoured the best crime books written by anyone living in Canada, or by a Canadian writing in another country.

Accomplishments

Carol continued to experiment with her writing. In 1993, her best known play, *Thirteen Hands*, was performed for the first time at a theatre in Winnipeg. The play is about elderly women who have played bridge together for years.

The same year, Carol had the biggest writing success of her career with the novel *The Stone Diaries*. The novel takes the form of a biography, but it is about a fictional character named Daisy. Daisy's life is described from her birth until old age. Many critics felt that Carol was able to make this woman's life seem as extraordinary as the life of any famous person.

The Stone Diaries won many prizes, including the Governor General's Award and the Pulitzer Prize. After the great success of the novel, many of Carol's earlier books were re-released in the United States and England.

Carol was the first Canadian to win the Pulitzer Prize for fiction in 1998.

Backgrounder

Pulitzer Prize

Pulitzer Prizes are awarded every year to Americans in the areas of **journalism**, letters, drama, and music. Prizes in the letters category include those for fiction, history, poetry, biography, and non-fiction. The awards are named after Joseph Pulitzer, an American newspaper publisher who was born in 1847. Carol Shields was eligible for a Pulitzer Prize because she is both a Canadian and an American citizen.

> " *We think we live full lives but in fact we live very narrow lives. We need more...I read [novels] to expand because I know how narrow my life is.* "

Carol has written eight novels, two short story, three poetry collections, and four plays in her more than twenty years as a professional writer.

Many people thought that Carol would feel a great deal of pressure to write a book that was even more popular than *The Stone Diaries*. She has never felt that she had to prove herself as a writer. As she has said, "I think every day when you sit down to write, you think maybe I can't do it today and will never do it again." Despite this, Carol continues to write steadily.

Larry's Party was Carol's next novel. It is written with a male lead character. During the time she was writing the novel, Carol became interested in mazes. The main character, Larry, is a gardener who specializes in designing mazes for gardens. The novel was a success.

In addition to her writing career, Carol has taught for many years as an English professor. She has always encouraged young writers to find their own voice. She and her husband plan to retire in Victoria, where Carol will continue to write.

▶▶▶▶▶▶

QUICK NOTES

▶ Carol and her husband have four daughters and one son.
▶ *Small Ceremonies*, Carol's first novel, was turned down by three publishers before it was finally accepted.
▶ Carol especially likes to write plays. She has said, "I feel I can do anything on stage."
▶ In 1998, Carol was diagnosed with cancer. She continued to write while in treatment.

MORE GREAT CANADIANS

Here are some more Canadians in literature. These accounts of their work will give you an idea of some of the ways literary artists can use their knowledge. The literary artists described here are only a few of the many. The Suggested Reading list will help you find more.

1920–
Pierre Berton

Pierre was born and raised in the Yukon and worked in mining camps while he was in university. He was later the managing editor of *Maclean's* magazine. He is also well known to Canadians for his many years on the television show *Front Page Challenge*.

Pierre writes non-fiction books about Canada and Canadian history. He has won three Governor General's Awards for creative non-fiction and was named a Companion of the Order of Canada in 1986. Over the years, Pierre has written fifty-six books and numerous plays, documentaries, and newspaper columns.

1960–
Douglas Cooper

Born in Toronto, Douglas published his first book, *Amnesia*, in 1992. His second novel, *Delirium*, was one of the first to be published in pieces on the Internet as it was being written. The book was later published in hardcover.

1961–
Douglas Coupland

Although Douglas did not invent the phrase Generation X, he made it popular with his first novel by the same name. *Generation X* quickly became a bestseller and captured the mood of young people in the early 1990s. He further explores pop culture in his other books, including *Shampoo Planet* and *Life After God*.

1930–
Timothy Findley

Although he began to write as a teenager, Timothy was best known as an actor for many years. He only began to take writing seriously when his friend and fellow actor Ruth Gordon encouraged him to write a story. Timothy has written many screenplays and novels including *The Wars*. In 1985, he was appointed an Officer of the Order of Canada.

Douglas Coupland

Anne Hébert

which was made into a movie. It addressed life on an Aboriginal reservation. Several of his plays have been performed in New York. In 1998, Tomson published his first novel. *Kiss of the Fur Queen* is partially based on Tomson's own life. In 1993, he was named a Member of the Order of Canada.

1931–

Rita Joe

Rita was born on an Aboriginal reserve in Cape Breton, Nova Scotia. After her mother died in 1937, Rita lived with various foster families. She has been writing poetry since the 1960s. Her poems are usually about the relationship that Aboriginal people have with Canadian society. Writing is Rita's way of expressing her private thoughts. As she travels Canada and the United States, she encourages the children she meets to write down their feelings. Rita was made a Companion of the Order of Canada in 1989.

1916–

Anne Hébert

In the 1950s, Anne wrote scripts for the National Film Board and worked on Radio-Canada broadcasts. She published her first collection of poetry in 1942. Her first novel, called *Le Torrent: Nouvelles*, was published in 1950, but it was not until 1970 that Anne's skill as a novelist was appreciated. Her novel *Kamouraska* brought her recognition and fame in both Canada and the United States. She is one of the best-known Québécois authors, and her works have been translated into English. Her books are read all over North America.

1951–

Tomson Highway

Born in a tent on a Cree reserve in Manitoba, Tomson had originally studied to become a classical pianist. He then began writing about the issues he knew best—being Aboriginal in Canada. Tomson has won many awards for his plays, including *The Rez Sisters*,

1935–

W.P. Kinsella

Bill's imaginative novels are known around the world. He returns to two different themes in many of his books. One is the experiences of the Aboriginal community in Canada. The second, which is the better known of the two, deals with baseball. One of Bill's most successful books, *Shoeless Joe*, was turned into the popular movie *Field of Dreams*. He went on to write *The Iowa Baseball Confederacy* in 1985. Bill has won many awards including the Stephen Leacock Medal in 1987, and he was named an Officer of the Order of Canada in 1993. "The secret of a fiction writer," says Bill, "is to make the dull interesting by imagination and embellishment, and to tone down the bizarre until it is believable."

1935–

Joy Kogawa

Joy's best-known work is *Obasan*, which was published in 1981. The book is based on her experiences as an interned Japanese Canadian during World War II. Before this book was released, Joy was a respected poet. Joy continued to write poetry and released a children's book called *Naomi's Road*. Joy was named a Member of the Order of Canada in 1986.

1932–

Jean Little

Jean has always had very poor eyesight, but her parents encouraged her to read. Her parents also encouraged her to write even when she was a child. Many of Jean's books are about children with physical challenges. She has written more than twenty books, including *Mama's Going to Buy You a Mockingbird*. Jean was appointed a Member of the Order of Canada in 1992.

Jean Little

Michael
Ondaatje

1958–

Ann-Marie MacDonald

Ann-Marie has always been a storyteller. She says the storytelling talents of her parents, both originally from Cape Breton, influenced her. Up until recently, Ann-Marie has been best known for her plays. She won a Governor General's Award for *Goodnight Desdemona (Good morning Juliet)*. In 1996, she wrote her first novel, *Fall On Your Knees*, which has since won many awards in Canada and elsewhere.

1914–1998

W.O. Mitchell

Born and raised in Saskatchewan, Bill was best known for his stories about life in small-town Canada. One of his best known books is *Who Has Seen the Wind*, published in 1947. The book was made into a successful movie in 1977. Many of his other novels, including *The Kite* in 1962, address similar questions about life and mortality.

Bill also wrote popular radio and television plays in the 1950s and 1960s. One of the most popular was *Jake and the Kid*, which started as pieces of fiction in *Maclean's* magazine.

Throughout his career, Bill has been awarded several honorary university degrees and writing awards. He was also named an Officer of the Order of Canada in 1973. Bill's writing has influenced writers across the country. He encouraged young writers in university programs through his position as writer-in-residence at several Canadian universities.

1943–

Michael Ondaatje

Born in Ceylon (now called Sri Lanka), Michael moved to Canada when he was nineteen years old. He began writing poetry. By 1971, he had won his first Governor General's Award for a book of poems entitled *The Collected Works of Billy the Kid*. Michael has written many popular novels. His 1992 book, *The English Patient*, won the Booker Prize. The book was made into a hit movie. Michael was named an Officer of the Order of Canada in 1988.

GLOSSARY

Alzheimer's disease: an illness that affects the brain. People suffering from the disease slowly lose their memory.

anthropology: the science of humans and human behaviour

autobiography: a book that an author writes about his or her own life

biography: a book written about another person's life

census: a collection of information about all the people in one area or the entire country

critics: writers who read books and then write articles containing their opinions of the books

endangered: when a species of animal is likely to become extinct unless something is done to save it

extinct: when all of one species of animal dies

fiction: writing, such as novels and short stories, that is imaginary. Fiction may be based on true events.

journalism: the work of writing, editing, managing, or publishing a newspaper, television news broadcast, or magazine

non-fiction: any writing, such as books, articles, or stories, that is true

manuscript: handwritten or typed text before it is published

oppression: the exercise of authority or power in a cruel or unjust manner

Parkinson's disease: an illness that affects the muscles in the body and slowly worsens them

primates: a group of animals that includes monkeys, apes, and humans

satirist: one who writes something that ridicules or makes fun of actions or values

scholarship: money that is given to a student, usually on the basis of high marks, to help pay for further education

science fiction: stories about what the future may be like

translate: to take a piece of writing in one language and rewrite it in another language

SUGGESTED READING

Authors & artists for young adults. Detroit: Gale Research, 1989.

Grant, Janet. *Kids' Writers.* Markham, Ontario: Fitzhenry & Whiteside, 1989.

Lang, Robert, ed. *Contemporary Canadian Authors.* Toronto: Gale Canada, 1996.

Major Authors and Illustrators for Children and Young Adults. Detroit: Gale Research, 1993.

Something about the author: facts and pictures about authors and illustrators of books for young people. Detroit: Gale Research, 1971.

Writing stories, making pictures: biographies of 150 Canadian children's authors and illustrators. Toronto: Canadian Children's Book Centre, 1994.

INDEX

Alias Grace 6, 10, 11
Alzheimer's disease 35, 46
anthropology 25, 46
Arctic 12, 14, 15, 17
autobiography 17, 35, 46

Canadian Armed Forces
    13
Canadian Broadcasting
    Corporation (CBC) 21,
    22, 36, 37
census 22, 46
Chatelaine 21
Circle Game, The 6, 9
critics 33, 39, 40, 46

day care 26, 27, 28

endangered 16, 46
extinct 16, 46

fiction 15, 22, 40, 44,
    45, 46
Fossey, Dian 12, 16

Giller Prize, The 6, 11, 18,
    23, 30, 35
Governor General's Award
    6, 9, 10, 11, 12, 15, 18,
    21, 22, 30, 36, 40, 42, 45
Grimm Brothers 7

Inuit 15

Jacob Two-Two 30, 33,
    34, 35
Jesuit 25, 26

Martchenko, Michael 27
Montgomery, Lucy Maud
    4, 19
Montreal 31, 32, 34, 35
Munro's Books 21

Nature Lore 13
Never Cry Wolf 12, 16
non-fiction 10, 34, 40,
    42, 46

Order of Canada 6, 9, 12,
    36, 42, 43, 44, 45
ornithology 13
Orthodox Jews 31

Paper Bag Princess, The
    24, 27
Parkinson's disease 19, 46
poetry 5, 7, 8, 9, 10, 11,
    19, 25, 36, 37, 38, 40, 41,
    43, 44, 45
primates 16, 46
Pulitzer Prize 36, 40

Québécois 34, 43

satirist 32, 46
scholarship 19, 46
science fiction 11, 25, 46
screenplay 30, 32, 42
separatists 34
Shoeless Joe 44
short stories 20, 21, 23,
    36, 39
Stone Diaries, The 36, 40,
    41
storytelling 17, 27, 29, 45

University of Toronto 6,
    8, 14

Vancouver Public Library
    20
Various Miracles 36, 39

wolves 14, 15, 16
writer-in-residence 22, 45